Nihil Obstat: Fr. Philip-Michael F. Tangorra, S.T.L.
Censor Librorum
Imprimatur: + Most Rev. Arthur J. Serratelli, S.T.D., S.S.L., D.D.
Bishop of Paterson
December 26, 2015

Text © 2016 by THE REGINA PRESS
an imprint of Catholic Book Publishing Corp.
77 West End Road
Totowa, NJ 07512

Illustrations: Marifé González
Illustrations © SUSAETA EDICIONES, S.A.
(RG14653)
ISBN: 978-0-88271-400-4   CPSIA February 2016   10 9 8 7 6 5 4 3 2 1   S/S
Printed in India
www.catholicbookpublishing.com

Preparing for
My First
Communion

Regina Press

Preparing for
My First Communion

ON the day you receive your First Communion, you receive the Holy Eucharist, the Sacrament of Jesus' Body and Blood. Jesus gives you Himself as holy food to nourish your soul.

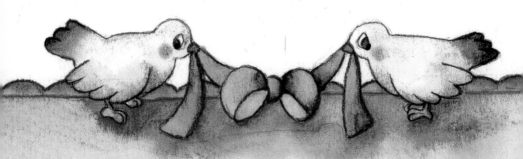

My Picture

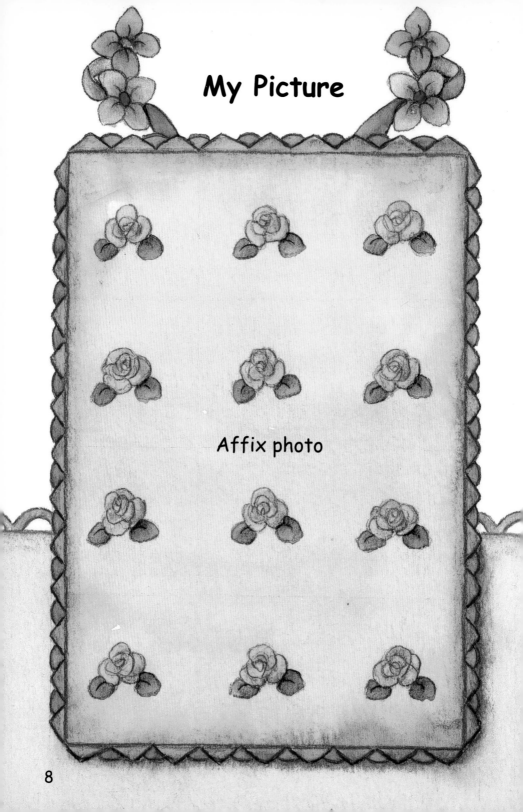

Affix photo

My name is..

....

I was born on ....

in ....

I was baptized on ....

I was baptized at...

....

I will make my First Communion at

....

I will make my First Communion on

....

Classmates with whom I will make my

First Communion are ....

....

....

The Priest who will give me my First

Communion is ....

Prayer

What is prayer?

PRAYER is talking to God and listening to Him in our heart so that we can learn what He wants us to do.

Why do we pray?

WE pray to adore God, to thank Him for His goodness, to seek His forgiveness, and to ask for His blessings.

How should we pray?

WE should pray with attention, with humility, with trust in God's goodness, and with all our heart.

Prayers for My First Communion

I believe in You, Jesus...

I BELIEVE in You, Jesus.
I believe that You are God and Man.
I believe that You came down from
heaven to show us the way
to Your Father.
I believe that You died for our sins
because You love us.

In Holy Communion...

IN Holy Communion, You come to me,
Jesus, to give life to my soul,
because You said that You are the
Bread of Life.

Jesus, make me more like You
through the grace of Holy Communion,
so that I may have
eternal life in heaven.

Prayer to the Virgin Mary

O MARY, Mother of Jesus,
and my dear Mother, too,
I honor and love you.

Blessed Mother most pure,
into your care I give
my body and soul;
keep them pure and holy.

Amen.

My Lord, My Savior

JESUS, I thank You
for having suffered and died
to make up for my sins
and to win grace for my soul.
I thank You for having opened
heaven to me by Your Death.

As You gave Your life for me,
may I live my life for You.

Prayer to Jesus

JESUS, I love You
in Holy Communion
when You give me
Your Body and Blood
as holy food for my soul.

Please give me Your grace
to help me be good
and stay away from evil.

Amen.

Help Me, Jesus

HELP me, Jesus, to follow You. Help me to be ready to make sacrifices to obey the Commandments of the Father and avoid sin.

Help me to serve God faithfully in this world.

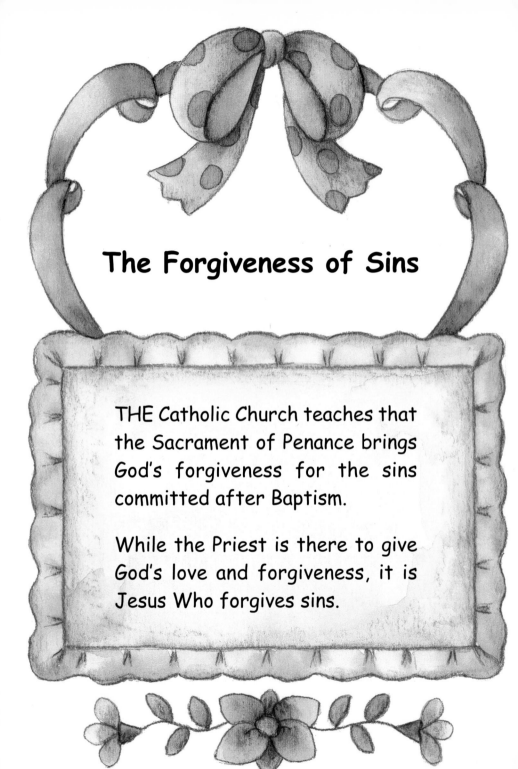

The Forgiveness of Sins

THE Catholic Church teaches that the Sacrament of Penance brings God's forgiveness for the sins committed after Baptism.

While the Priest is there to give God's love and forgiveness, it is Jesus Who forgives sins.

Confession

WHEN you receive the Sacrament of Penance, it is very important that you:

1° Ask how you have offended God.

2° Be truly sorry for your sins.

3° Make up your mind not to sin again.

4° Tell your sins to the Priest.

5° Do the penance the Priest gives you.

21

Prayer before Confession

MY dearest Jesus, I have sinned. Help me to say to the Priest what I say to You in the secret of my heart. Help me be truly sorry for having offended You or someone else. Help me to make up for my sins and to try to do better.

Prayer after Confession

MY dearest Jesus, I have told all my sins as well as I could. I have tried hard to make a good Confession. I thank You because I feel sure that You have forgiven me. Without You, I could not be freed from my sins. Thank You for Your love and mercy.

Cross

JESUS died on the Cross because of His love for us.

The Sign of the Cross expresses two important mysteries of our Faith: the Blessed Trinity and Jesus opening the gates of heaven by His Death and Resurrection.

When do I make the Sign of the Cross?

—Whenever I enter or leave a church.

—Whenever I begin or finish saying a prayer.

—Whenever I pass a church.

Christian

A PERSON who accepts the teachings of Jesus Christ.

Eucharist

THE word Eucharist means
"thanksgiving."

Sacrilege

THE treatment of sacred persons, places, or things with disrespect.

pom
pom

Penance

PRAYERS or good works assigned by the Priest after one has confessed his or her sins.

Gospel

THE "good news" of and about Jesus Christ.

Alleluia!

AN expression of praise and joy.

The Bible

THE Bible is the inspired Word of God. It is divided into the Old Testament, which has 46 Books and the New Testament, which has 27 Books. The Old Testament points toward man's need for a Redeemer because of his sinfulness, as shown in the story of Jonah and the whale. The New Testament tells of our Redeemer, Jesus Christ.

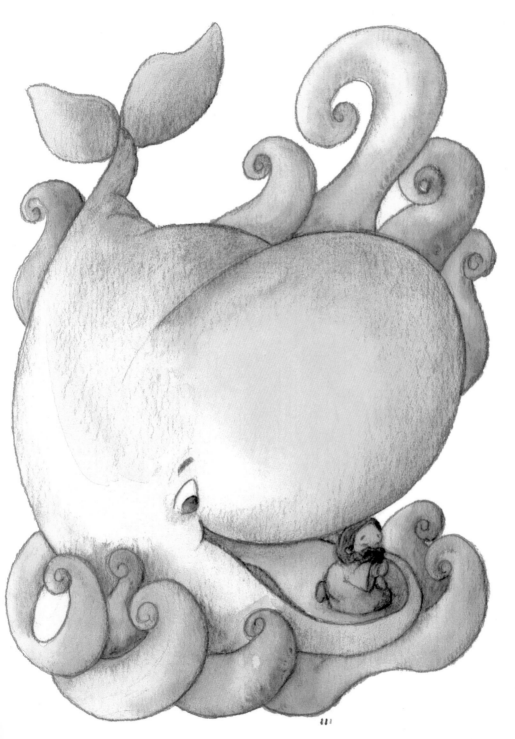

The 7 Deadly Sins

Pride

Greed

Lust

Anger

Gluttony

Envy

Sloth

The Virtues against
the Deadly Sins

Against pride, humility.

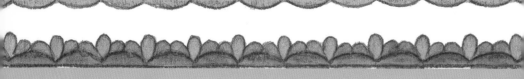

Against greed, generosity.

Against lust, purity.

Against anger, patience.

Against gluttony, moderation.

Against envy, charity.

Against sloth, diligence.

Readings

IT is important to listen to the readings not only at your First Communion Mass, but at every Mass.

The Commandments

THERE are 10 Commandments that God gave to Moses on Mount Sinai:

1. I AM the Lord, your God. You shall not have strange gods before Me.

2. YOU shall not take the name of the Lord, your God, in vain.

3. REMEMBER to keep holy the Sabbath.

4. YOU shall honor your father and your mother.

5. YOU shall not kill.

6. YOU shall not commit adultery.

7. YOU shall not steal.

8. YOU shall not bear false witness against your neighbor.

9. YOU shall not covet your neighbor's wife.

10. YOU shall not covet your neighbor's goods.

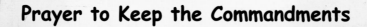

Prayer to Keep the Commandments

DEAR God,
please help me to love and serve
You always.
I pray that I will honor and
respect Your name.
Help me to love the Mass and to
attend Mass every Sunday as a
perfect act of worship.

I ask Your help to obey my parents
and to be sorry when
I disobey them.
I pray that I will not become angry
with anyone.
Guide me so that I will be pure and
modest in thought,
word, and deed.

Please help me to be fair
and not to take what doesn't
belong to me.
I pray that I will speak truthfully
and not say unkind or false things
about anyone.

Guide my thoughts and actions
so that they always will
be pure.
Help me to not want what others
have and to be happy with all You
have given me.